I Like Animals

by Muriel L. Dubois

Consultant:
Barbara M. Parramore
Professor Emeritus, Curriculum and Instruction
North Carolina State University

Bridgestone Books
an imprint of Capstone Press
Mankato, Minnesota

Bridgestone Books are published by Capstone Press
151 Good Counsel Drive, P.O. Box 669, Mankato, Minnesota 56002
http://www.capstone-press.com

Library of Congress Cataloging-in-Publication Data
Dubois, Muriel L.
  I like animals: what can I be?/by Muriel L. Dubois.
    p. cm.—(What can I be?)
  Includes bibliographical references and index.
  Summary: Describes various careers working with animals and what they involve,
including animal groomer, pet store owner, and veterinarian.
  ISBN 0-7368-0630-X
  1. Animal specialists—Vocational guidance—Juvenile literature. [1. Animal specialists.
2. Occupations.] I. Title. II. Series.
SF80 .D83 2001
636'.0023—dc21   00-021617

Editorial Credits

Tom Adamson, editor; Heather Kindseth, designer; Katy Kudela, photo researcher

Photo Credits

Bob Daemmrich/Pictor, 16
Ed Elberfeld/Pictor, cover (bottom inset)
Index Stock Imagery, 6
Inga Spence/TOM STACK & ASSOCIATES, cover, 10
James P. Rowan, 18
John Clobes, 8
John Decre/Pictor, 14
Kent and Donna Dannen, 20
Kent Knudson/Pictor, cover (middle inset)
Kevin Syms/Pictor, 4
Root Resources/Richard Jacobs, cover (top inset)
Visuals Unlimited, 12

1 2 3 4 5 6 06 05 04 03 02 01

Table of Contents

People Who Enjoy Animals

You may like to read books about animals. Maybe you care for a pet or watch birds in your yard. You might like to visit zoos or aquariums. You can have a job working with animals when you grow up.

Animal Groomer

Animal groomers help keep pets clean and healthy. Groomers trim dogs' and cats' claws. They wash, brush, and cut the animals' fur. Groomers know special styles for some pets. They may need to keep nervous pets calm.

Pet Store Owner

Pet store owners sell birds, fish, cats, dogs, and other animals. They also sell food, cages, and toys for different pets. Pet store owners need to know how to care for the pets they sell. They answer questions for new pet owners.

Animal Trainer

Different kinds of trainers work with animals. Some animal trainers teach dogs to work with police officers. Some animal trainers teach pets how to behave. Others train animals to do tricks for shows. Some train dogs to guide people who are blind.

Biologist

Biologists are scientists who study animals in their natural habitats. Biologists work to protect endangered animals. Some biologists study certain kinds of animals. Marine biologists study ocean life. Ornithologists study birds.

endangered
a kind of animal that is close to dying out

Livestock Farmer

Livestock farmers raise animals for food. These farmers work to produce healthy hens, sheep, pigs, or cows. They give each animal the right food. They clean the animals' living areas. They care for sick animals.

livestock
animals raised on a farm

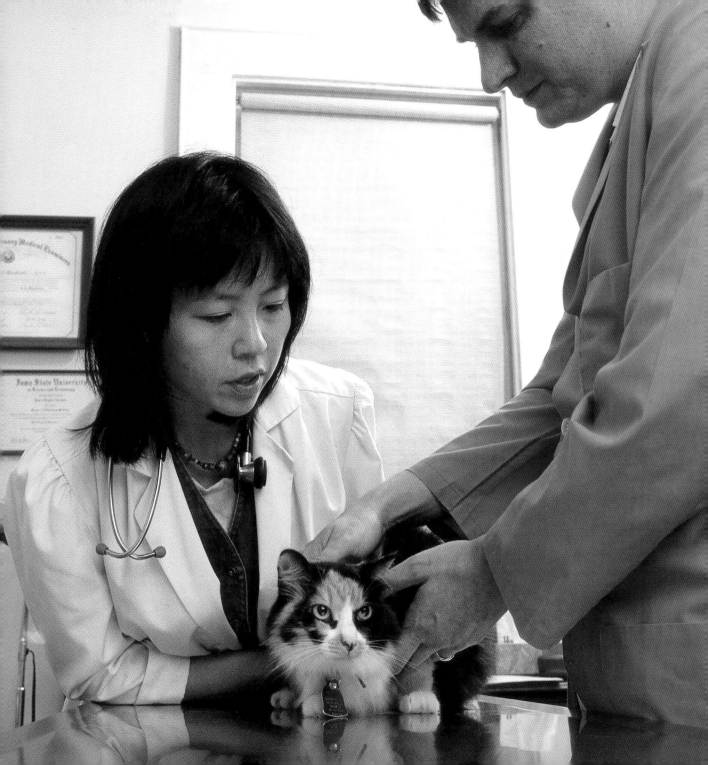

Veterinarian

Veterinarians are doctors who treat animals. Most veterinarians treat pets in animal hospitals. Others care for large animals that live on farms or in zoos. Veterinarians give shots and set broken bones. They help people keep their animals healthy.

Zookeeper

Zookeepers work with animals that live in zoos. Zookeepers feed the animals and keep their habitats clean. They care for sick animals and baby animals. Some zookeepers also work to save endangered animals.

Preparing to Work with Animals

You can prepare for a career in animal care. Take care of a pet. Volunteer with an adult at an animal shelter. Read books about animals. You can learn about animals in science classes.

volunteer
to offer to do a job without pay

Hands On: Make a Model Zoo

What You Need

Index cards
Crayons
Books about zoo animals
Wooden craft sticks (at least 20)
White glue
Masking tape

What You Do

1. Fold one index card in half. Draw a picture of a zoo animal on one side. The folded card helps your animal stand.
2. Read about the animal. Write the animal's name and two facts about the animal on another card.
3. Place three craft sticks on a table side by side about 1 inch (2.5 centimeters) apart.
4. Put a dot of glue on the end of each craft stick.
5. Glue a craft stick across the top. Glue another craft stick across the bottom. This is one wall of your habitat.
6. Repeat steps 3 through 5 to make three more walls.
7. Use masking tape to join the inside of the walls. The walls should form a box shape like the picture above.
8. Put your animal inside its habitat. Place the facts about the animal next to the habitat.
9. Add more animals to your zoo. Give a friend a tour of your zoo. Tell your friend about the animals.

Words to Know

aquarium (uh-KWAIR-ee-uhm)—a place where people can see or study live fish and ocean life

biologist (bye-OL-uh-jist)—a scientist who studies living things

habitat (HAB-uh-tat)—the place and natural conditions where an animal usually lives

hospital (HOSS-pi-tuhl)—a place that gives medical treatment; some veterinarians work in animal hospitals.

ornithologist (or-nuh-THOL-uh-jist)— a biologist who studies birds

veterinarian (vet-ur-uh-NER-ee-uhn)—a doctor who treats sick or injured animals

Read More

Deedrick, Tami. *Zoo Keepers*. Community Helpers. Mankato, Minn.: Bridgestone Books, 1998.

Flanagan, Alice. *Dr. Friedman Helps Animals*. Our Neighborhood. New York: Children's Press, 2000.

Lee, Barbara. *Working with Animals*. Exploring Careers. Minneapolis: Lerner, 1996.

Internet Sites

National Wildlife Federation
http://www.nwf.org/nwf/kids
National Zoo
http://www.si.edu/natzoo

Index